I Am the Bitter Name

BY C. K. WILLIAMS

Lies
I Am the Bitter Name

C. K. Williams

I Am the Bitter Name

HOUGHTON MIFFLIN COMPANY BOSTON 1972

First Printing W

ISBN: 0–395–13527–3 Hardbound
ISBN: 0–395–13528–1 Paperbound
Library of Congress Catalogue Card Number: 71–170161

Printed in the United States of America

The following poems were first published in *The Major Young Poets*,
edited by Al Lee and published by World Publishing Company, 1971:
"This Is a Sin" (under the title "This Poem Is a Sin"), "The Nickname
of Hell," "I Am the Bitter Name," "The Kingdom of Stinking Wishes,"
"Agencies Portions Crying," "How Humble We Were Before This," "Becoming
Somebody Else," "This Day," and "The Nut."

Other poems have appeared in the following periodicals: *American Poetry
Review*, "In the Heart of the Beast"; *Iowa Review*, "Bringing It Home" and
"The Spirit the Triumph"; *Ironwood*, "The Little Shirt" and "Then the
Brother of the Wind"; *Lillabulero*, "Another Dollar" and "They Warned Him";
The New American Review, "Yours" and "The Rabbit Fights for Its
Life the Leopard Eats Lunch"; *The New Yorker*, "Keep It"; *Poetry*, "Innings,"
"Clay Out of Silence," "The Undead," and "The Rampage";
Transpacific Review, "A Poem for the Governments."

for my mother and father

III.

IV.

I

"Which is the serpent that flies in the air and walks alone, and meanwhile an ant resting between its teeth has the enjoyment, beginning in community and ending in isolation?"

A POEM FOR THE GOVERNMENTS

this poem is an onion
it's the same one miguel hernandez'
wife wrote him about in jail
before he died that there was nothing
else for her and the baby to eat
except onions so he wrote
a lullaby for the child about onions
"I awoke from being a child:
don't you awake . . . don't even know
what happens or what goes on"

this poem is an onion
for you mr old men because
I want tears from you now
and can't see how else to get them
I want tears for miguel now
for the poor people and their children
and for the kids you hate going
around cunt-frontwards full of carrying on
and bad shit like mercy and despair
I offer this

because everything else with life
and tenderness in it you've eaten
everything good in the world eaten
everything in my heart eaten
the poor eaten the babies eaten miguel
eaten
now eat this: this is one onion
your history and legacy
it is all there is in our lives
this and tears: eat this

ANOTHER DOLLAR

I dreamed of an instrument of political torture
so that the person thinks he's breathing into a great space
that flows like a river beyond men
into infinity the ethical disconnects like a phone
and what he says everything comes back to him WE ARE NOT
  DOING THIS
angels skulls prisoners WE ARE NOT DOING THIS
the children scouring themselves like genitals NOT DOING THIS

mother am I the enemy or the little brother?
they threw ropes around me I ran I covered myself
but they touched me the invalids licked me the poor kissed me
afterwards there is a bed afterwards a woman is there
her breasts she is a cloud how she envelops you
the coils shimmer nobody talks anymore nobody dreams this
WE ARE NOT DOING THIS

THE BEGINNING OF APRIL

I feel terribly strong today
it's like the time I arm-wrestled a friend
and beat him so badly I sprained his wrist
or when I made a woman who was really beautiful
love me when she didn't want to
it must be the warm weather
I think
I could smash bricks with my bare hands
or screw
until I was half out of my mind

the only trouble
jesus the only trouble
is I keep thinking about a kid I saw starving on television
last night from biafra he was unbearably fragile
his stomach puffed up arms and legs sticks eyes distorted
what if I touched somebody like that when I was this way?
I can feel him going stiff under my hands
I can feel his belly bulging ready to pop
his pale hair disengaging from its roots like something
    awful and alive
please

I won't hurt you I want you in my arms
I want to make something for you to eat like warm soup
look I'll chew the meat for you first
in case your teeth ache
I'll keep everybody away if you're sleeping
and hold you next to me like a little brother when we go out
I'm so cold now
what are we going to do with all this?
I promise I won't feel myself like this ever again
it's just the spring it doesn't mean anything please

THIS IS A SIN

right off we started inflicting history
on each other day after day first thing this
is historical and we gave dollars for it
and this and we gave movies and sad poems
and obviously newspapers and a little less
valentines and sometimes it got right
up against us and into us we would squeeze
it out like a worm it would come back
by itself through the pancreas through
the eye or womb and with great tenderness
on the faces of wives and babies we
would reinflict it until there was
such beauty it was unbearable because
it was too much history too much suffering
and also birds suffering their leaps
from branches dogs
lifting their dark mouths the paths
of mantises cows plopping were we afraid
of what would be left of us? sometimes
a person was erased entirely
and children dead of shame stuck
upright in the snow like pipes the wind
screaming over them or I would forget
you darling your breasts the wind
over them our lips
moving darling the child the wind breasts
our lips over them

THE UNDEAD

the only way it makes sense
is that we have terrible wounds inside us like mouths hard
metallic made in america
they swing fatly open like wallets and gorge
in strict vaginal contractions what touches us
what comes to us living wants us

how many times the one we kiss with affirms LIFE! LIFE!
but the other when the saints said
they heard thunder it was just it closing and
this time when it opens corpses soar in it officers
at attention shells
this time not enough pain in all asia for it

I want you not comforting me
the soles of our feet beaten until worms of flesh erupt from
    them
our genitals dialed like wrong numbers don't
put your tongue in me don't give me anything heart
soul laughter anything children turning the light on and off
on and off MA! don't feed me! don't feed me!

WHAT MUST I DO TO BE LOST?

what I am now is the cock
of some infinite animal stiffening
and softening like a planet
in the spaces beyond kiss
before he had me
my animal pushed his face into the end and kept going
life rode him there
was no one he hadn't torn to pieces
my animal clicks back and forth and smokes
he wants to go through us now out of the universe
like both moons
he wants to cough into the sanctuaries bleed
on the risers shrivel
the fruits of our soul in his centuries
love pony darling let
me be fields mines dry ditches
my animal opens I
sway I thrust aimlessly nothing
is mine here
take the knife I can't here
swim in the thick break
me darling
I am nailed in like a root
meat

THEN THE BROTHER OF THE WIND

there's no such thing as death everybody
knows that also
nothing in the world that can batter you
and hang you on a fencepost like a towel

and no such thing as love that stays inside
getting thicker and heavier falling
into the middle one seed
that weighs more than the universe

and no angels either
and even if there were even if we hadn't laughed
the second heart out and made the second brain
have whole wars happening inside it like bacteria

and if they were made out of tin cans like shacks
in rio and rubber tires like crete sandals
and were all the same place rags in ratholes
in harlem rags sticking to burned faces in bengal

we'd still break like motors
and slip out of them anyway like penises
onto the damp thigh
and have to begin over

LIKE LITTLE BIRDS

I'm sick and tired of sharing
everything with everybody I want a number of my own now
like god has with his name just me knowing it nobody
else unless I tell them
it's why there's money isn't it? we get a pile
start counting finish get
another still
wrong like god and the letters he puts death
onto life then life on top then love mixes them up throws them
  down
shuffles them picks them up one at a time then handfuls
bleeding

god what
I'll do now is lie down here and count backwards
and you'll tell me when
right? but god not
before zero this time it's dark
here you can't see
it's like a coffin things crawl in with you
take nibbles but you don't feel them
my poor number god I don't care
for myself but family friends government god
for their sake not here again

THE NEXT TO THE LAST POEM ABOUT GOD

when jessie's fever went up god got farther away so he could
    see better
he wanted to know everything that happened
when I hit tex my brother in the face with a cap gun
when I ran away from my mother and had a bad fight
with my sister lynn about being different
when I dreamed of being a fighter pilot and shooting my father
    down
god was there in my dream too think how big he had to be
to get in where I was sailing around in my flying tiger
and the deaf kid he was in his ears somebody told me so it was
    all right
and jimmy moss when he died it was autumn there were leaves
outside the window just hardening I thought
he must be in the leaves too how big he is how far away
he must be to cover everything like a blanket
you crawl in with a fever and hide and wake up some time
during the night all better and crawl out again
but maybe when he has to get that far he thins out a little
you know? like rubber? maybe sometimes people punch
their fingers through him by accident or maybe on purpose
the bad people because they wanted to see everything too
because seeing everything would be like owning everything
so they go through and there they were bouncing around
saying everything's good everything figures it all works
you could see them walking across the sky
at night rippling the cover making the stars bend
they said come up here look you can see EVERYTHING! EVERY-
    THING!
tex I'm sorry I hit you in the face
mom I didn't mean to grow up you should have told me lynn
dad forgive me for getting stronger
sally you for so much and jessie

when you were playing on the bed last night
letting yourself fall backwards onto me with such happy trust
thinking "stand up" meant "let yourself fall any way you want to
I'll catch you" jessie you were almost well your fever
was almost gone and I thought there must be something
    important
for you like that I still can't think of it but god must know it
because god doesn't forget anything ever
and someday I'll get that far too and find out
and drop messages about what it was and it'll be all right
god told me he said tell jessie I said it'll be all right

ACIDS

FOR JEFF MARKS

something to dip myself into
like sheep when they're driven through
and the ticks and fleas float off in the trough
the animals struggling to keep their heads out of it
the men dunking them for their own good they get fatter the
    wool thicker
I would come up
crying
but pure again fingerprints kissmarks the places
I crossed my arms and dug into my back invisible
scales imperceptible bony emotional excrescences
gone a caul
gleaming flushing the surfaces innocence
I would make rivers of it
that would flood at their mouths
and the swimmers
would be done too
and in the city in the tap water
enough scum left to get into us all
we would fall into great laughing heaps of ourselves
can you imagine laughter
shining
and the sounds of lovemaking
etched like printing plates
so you would pull pictures of being young and knowing
what you know now
the first sky the first clouds
like young angels
bumping each other seeing your mother coming shrieking
joyfully so she'll hear you
and come running arms open face open baby!
baby!
and you

flowing being flowed through
like the blood
over the skull then
the veil and before that in your arms
in all of you

THEY WARNED HIM THEN THEY THREW HIM AWAY

there's somebody who's dying
to eat god
when the name happens
the juices leap from the bottom of his mouth like waves
he almost falls over with lightheadedness
nobody has ever been this hungry before
you might know people who've never had anything
but teaspoons of rice or shreds
from the shin of an ape well that's nothing
you should know what this person would do
he'd pull handfuls of hair out of his children
and shove them down
he'd squeeze the docile bud in his wife
until it screamed
if you told him god lived in his own penis
he'd bite into it
and tear like a carnivore
this is how men renounce
this is how we obliterate
one morning near the end he'll climb into the fire
and look back at himself
what was dark will be light
what was song will be roaring
and the worst thing is you'll still want this
beyond measure you'll still want this
believe me
you should know this

PORTIONS OF MANSLAYER

my face ends inside you
it goes in on the tip
I am rushing into it
from behind where my back is
in the darkness and I want
to be this close nothing between us
the stripes burn there are just wisps
I go through where they were time
washes me like clear water and you
are in my face
inside too
but you say SAVE ME
you say GO BACK
well
this stinks
this face
the world is inside this face but it's lousy
remember you used to say MAKE A FACE
MAKE A FACE
for you
only
in the blood where you can't tell anyway
I'm making them
I whisper look! look!
but there's no world
I'm not in this face not this one
it stinks
it's just nothing

AGENCIES PORTIONS CRYING

my friends are all going away to have
fun without even knowing it's the police
who've handed out pictures of islands
and beautiful women they were reading
the paper and there it was the big
voice fell saying come on the fingers
tickled them and what the hell they
said what's the difference except me
because what I was told was stay here!
you stay! and I'm too lonely to bury
the bad pieces under the bed I'm
too sad to boil the grief down heavier
nothing is true anymore I haven't
used up like a bad book I made it
do things but suppose without you I turn
blue like a policeman my badge finding
its eagle my boots marching left
right I would see your body tied down
I would remember us laughing together
and you turning away still laughing and
the policeman who I am and the jury
we would kill you because we missed you
so much we would warn you be good or else
die and you wouldn't and o shit death
again at the end of the film
rage still nobody here listening

A HEART FOR THE FATHERS

FOR STEVE BERG

nobody's all love
so god cured a few cripples brought some corpses back
and they said god you bastard
and god said
furious doesn't count
and they said god
you cocksucker
and god said tenderness either

nobody's all hate either
if you want to cure somebody
maybe the only way is murdering them if you don't
kill them anyway they're no good

he said LOOK! SPRING! they threw their guns down
he said SUNSETS! they took their teeth out
and made bullets
DAUGHTERS! that was too much
they killed him too

so nobody's still all
one thing or another we go
around laying hands on and nothing happens
except death again and you ask them again and
they say no
fair again it doesn't count

JETSAM

I'm being punished this time for crying
too much and because I used to inflict
pain on everybody I loved without knowing
it and so everything's finished the carburetor
I carried around tuning the single flower
the sink tap the window starting to murmur
where's charity? I can't think
of anything but the words for you bar
bedpost house I keep disappearing
in the holes where my voice was and
what I have by myself now this tube
in my left hand this meat in my tearing
right nobody knows
but the last man with rubbers pulled down
over his face who's me too it's night
his eyelids stop tears from
both ways so if somebody cried out loud
he'd call it compassion if there was nothing
ever again he'd say that's right desire

RIBBONS

the goddamned animals might know more than we do about
   some things
like looking away when somebody they know is hurting them
and the other has to let go and not tear his throat out like us
but we're still more than them about love
a girl so shy she couldn't look at me without crying
so I turned the other way too and you could feel how close we
   were
as though we'd circled the whole world
and met and fallen in love her legs smoothed
I was stronger there were mists we walked in them

now when does that happen with pigs or horses?
the stallion all he's after is tearing the fence down
the mare gets her tail going like a pump handle
and in the paddock the gelding old sergeant
buries his face in the creaky feed bin and keeps it there
remembering iwo jima remembering the bulge seoul my lai
his wound his two thighs like medals his two thighs
rising into the dark like searchlights only animals would keep
   quiet then
grind their broad teeth on the grain and shut up not us

THE NUT

a man hammers viciously
viciously like fucking
a bad whore who won't get
undressed even remember?
like trying to crush
the life from the corpse who
sprays blood who won't
die or stop screaming
until the mouth is gone
utterly the last thread
crawling tenderly down
the backbone tenderly
to the tail the legs men
what are we thinking
hammering? the poor whore
smashing her fists on
the wall the carpenter his
sensitive tools suffering
men the terrible claws
men the hammering not
sleeping the hammering
going on to eternity
what is this so much
like pulse like murdering?
the corpse screams the
woman screams men what
is this?

YOURS

I'd like every girl in the world to have a poem of her own
I've written for her I don't even want to make love to them all
    anymore
just write things your body makes me delirious your face
    enchants me
you are a wonder of soul spirit intelligence one for every one
and then the men I don't care whether I can still beat them all
them too a poem for them how many?
seeing you go through woods like part of the woods seeing you
    play piano
seeing you hold your child in your tender devastating hands
and of course the children too little poems they could sing or
    dance to
this is our jumping game this our seeing game our holding each
    other
even the presidents with all their death the congressmen and
    judges
I'd give them something
they would hold awed to their chests as their proudest life thing
somebody walking along a road where there's no city would
    look up
and see his poem coming down like a feather out of nowhere
or on the assembly line new instructions a voice sweet as
    lunchtime
or she would turn over a stone by the fire and if she couldn't
    read
it would sing to her in her body
listen! everyone! you have your own poem now
it's yours as much as your heart as much as your own life is
you can do things to it shine it up iron it dress it in doll clothes
o men! o people! please stop how it's happening now please
I'm working as fast as I can I can't stop to use periods

sometimes I draw straight lines on the page because the words
are too slow
I can only do one at a time don't die first please
don't give up and start crying or hating each other they're
    coming
I'm hurrying be patient there's still time isn't there? isn't there?

II

*"And Abraham said to him, 'And art thou, indeed, he
that is called Death?'
He answered, and said, 'I am the Bitter Name.'"*

I AM THE BITTER NAME

the little children have been fighting
a long long time for their beloved country
their faces are hardening like meat
left out their bodies squashed flat
like flowers in lawbooks don't fit
with the keys to eternal sorrow anymore
is the best toy always death? everyone
crying in the sleepy hair inexhaustible
agony in the dark cups of the skull
unquenchable agony your hands shriek
on my spine like locked brakes in
the torn nostrils tendrils in the mouth
vines the little soldiers play
wounding the little generals play hurt
forever they sharpen things they put
things in things they pull them out
will you make freedom for me? in
the cheekbone fire in the lips my
justice is to forget being here my liberty
wanting to hate them how they are shipped
home in ice-cream bags and being able to

KEEP IT

the lonely people are marching
on the capital everyone's yelling not
to give them anything but just
buying dinner together was fun
wasn't it? don't give them a thing
the boss said the boss
is dreaming of beautiful nurses
the lonely people are taking
all their little dogs to washington
back home the channels change
by themselves the soap changes
to perfume perfume to cereal the boss
dreams of the moon landing on
spruce street nobody is lonely
on locust nobody is left
at all the sun comes by himself
the buses go along by themselves
and wonder have I told you about
my disease? the lonely people
hold tight at night
on the coast they are tucked
in under the twilight
together the boss walks
across them it was fun it was
so much fun wasn't it?

THE SPIRIT THE TRIUMPH

do you remember learning to tie your shoes?
astonishing! the loops you had to make the delicate
adjustments the pulling-through tightening impossible!
the things we learn!
putting a bridle on a horse when he's headshy
getting your hands under a girl's sweater
no wonder we are the crown of all that exists
we can do anything how we climb chimneys
how we put one foot on the gas one on the clutch
and make the car go nothing too difficult nothing!

crutches artificial arms have you seen that?
how they pick their cups up and use razors? amazing!
and the wives shine it for them at night
they're sleeping the wives take it out of the room
and polish it with its own special rag
it's late they hold it against their bellies
the leather laces dangle into their laps
the mechanisms slip noiselessly
lowering the hook softly onto their breasts
we men! aren't we something? I mean
we are worth thinking about aren't we?
we are the end we are the living end

HOW HUMBLE WE WERE BEFORE THIS

what if the ethical gunmen isolated evil
out of death and all there was left was screaming
I hate you at each other the targets
licked clean the ground white as aspirin we weren't
sacrificed to the golden sorrow we didn't win
prizes for suffering did we? I
am so sorry for us picture
this you are dragging me
through the front lines your velvety guts
string out on wires your face transfigures
with concentration but I come back
I cry harder and echoes how
are you what's new kiss me fuck me love
me are there anyway right? ponies
with scarlet shoulders right? prisoners
lullabying our sore breath with ashes?
everything we left out everything
we were afraid of is jammed back
in us like gigantic numbers swollen
with wanting killing with wanting being
alive without killing but always vengeance
I nail the dimes back I bite harder
than dear life what it is to be empty
what it is without passion there
is nothing like this being sanctified

MADDER

"People can screw dead bodies, but they never feed them."

the nations have used up their desire
the cunts of the mothers the cunts
of the bad daughters stinking
of police stations of the sisters
and generations of old men saying
look cunt what about me saying look
cunt how I'm bleeding saying cunt cunt
where is forgiveness? what bullshit

you can kiss me good-bye but first put
your hands up let me search you
first good-bye I'll check your rectum
for poison and recite how we spoiled
from the inside like lettuce I'll tell
about freedom vomited on our foreheads
I'll say LOOK WHAT YOU DID and men
reading money aloud laughing aloud

I'm fed up with the sugars of raw
human flesh cursing I gallop over her
with my nicked tongue head to toe
I plow in with my notched cock cursing
the suffering of labels the
suffering of elegant canned goods of
mercy vengeance witness borne
for no end the governments are silent

or I'm dying of grief and loving both
ends of it or of solace and mixing
up whether we're here at all and revenge
or peace and who did it first dear

husbands dear wives tighter they're
washing my mouth out with soap I promise
not to accuse you but this time you
be the secret this time you comfort me

POOR HOPE

which is worse the lieutenant raising his rifle
toward the astonished women and children jammed
into the bomb-crater raising it not even aiming just carelessly
beginning to do it the way you'd rake a lawn you start
anywhere that or when I saw a boy in a department store
with his mother he was skipping along going toot toot toot
when the mother saw me I could see her flinch about something
and when I passed them she cracked him him! not me
across the mouth stunning him terribly hissing
don't you know where you are? which is worse
to be in the world with that or with that? or is it
that there's god and you think they've killed him!
then the dread god did you really say hit them! kill them!
then to the children then the mothers forgive me then myself
    then
nothing no sacrament for the people forgotten
in mid-sentence gone except in fuck you! where they cry god
I have thought two ways up the first
is when I felt the boy's spirit become pain because of me
I should have apologized not to him or even the mother
but to YOU! I'm sorry and the other is for the others
in the ditch in their torn clothes just as the bullets go into them
I would go mad and have you seen how men in toilets
at stadiums or the movies stare into the wall
so we won't covet each other's cocks? I would stare
into you like that and never move again never let you die
again never let you be anywhere else staring watching
you boil helplessly back and forth on the ceiling
don't move! trying to electrocute yourself on the wires
stay where you are! trying to slice your body
to pieces on the fluttering cobwebs don't die on me!

BRINGING IT HOME

a room all the way across america
and a girl in the room and the plastic fattening her breasts
starting to sag o god
she thinks they're going o god o god
I would do anything to help her
I would take all of her secret pain onto myself if she'd let me
my best darling
it is your soul melting it
it is the fire in you

I remember fire
everywhere in the world
boys scratching two sticks together so proud of themselves
houses going up in spontaneous combustion or somebody using
    his lighter
and the girl locked in in back still touching her fearful body
(you too my best darling)
and furnaces men with sweat stung out of them
faces cooked broiled smoked while they make things for us

and in america
in her breasts the two fires
like gods the two fires without flame
and her voice this flame rising out of my throat
it says FUCK YOU I DON'T CARE
it says UP YOUR ASS TOO YOU WEIRD FAGGOTS
my best darling my best darling

THE LITTLE SHIRT

what we need is one of those gods
who comes howling down streets
like a police car into the houses into
the television sets the refrigerators
comes oozing through everything and eats
everything everything the whole box
the darkness the dust
under the stairs the roaches and then us
and then makes us up again
out of her wonderful mouth earth
so that we look into our friends suddenly understanding
flesh how it tightens and lets go
to have this pass through
to be able to blink so that it goes through
to be able to get back from this
so mother death will be happy
so we won't hurt her she
keeps her big hand on us her thighs over our heads
she jumps we fall out like apples
and having to own her
and having to have war for her and fucking
and thankfulness so she won't stink in her people
we believe her
cloudlife airlife scent the
flavors to lick off
going up firing back at ourselves
make me sergeant! get me a hard-on!
to kill
never to go from this

CLAY OUT OF SILENCE

chances are we will sink quietly back
into oblivion without a ripple
we will go back into the face
down through the mortars as though it hadn't happened

earth: I'll remember you
you were the mother you made pain
I'll grind my thorax against you for the last time
and put my hand on you again to comfort you

sky: could we forget?
we were the same as you were
we couldn't wait to get back sleeping
we'd have done anything to be sleeping

and trees angels for being thrust up here
and stones for cracking in my bare hands
because you foreknew
there was no vengeance for being here

when we were flesh we were eaten
when we were metal we were burned back
there was no death anywhere but now
when we were men when we became it

INNINGS

somebody keeps track of how many times
I make love don't you god don't you?
and how good it is telling me
it's marked down where I can't see
right underneath me so the next time
something unreal happens in the papers
I don't understand it it doesn't touch
me I start thinking
everyone's heart might be pure
after all because what the hell
they don't kill me just each other
they don't actually try making me sad
just do things make things happen
suffer things I erupt
into the feminine like a lion don't
I god? among doves? so even being with me
is like beauty? I move under this god
like a whore I gurgle I roll
like a toy boat what's the score
now god? am I winning?

CREAMS

put mommy on the front steps
with her legs open and baby all
grown up hers too every morning
they'd tangle their pants off
and go out crying every
morning the soldiers
would be there washing themselves
like socks and the good part
would be breezes licking
in sparrows packed up in cartons
but the bad part again after
all this the children born
with self-addressed tags HOME
DARLING MY SORROW lashing
them like wings their voices
hurting them their hearts
trying to quench the hideous
laughter forgive
us we were alone for a long
time like this nothing would tell
us what was wrong and it
was delicious anyway being
blamed wanting to want too
much and being banged back
to the life again we tried
everything sweethearts we tried
the last thing and then this
death by itself then this

BECOMING SOMEBODY ELSE

your lists of victims dear
god like rows of sharp little teeth
have made me crazy look
I have crushed my poor balls
for you I have kissed the blank
pages drunk the pissy chalice
water and thrown up dear god your
rabbits dear god your big
whistle do you know how awful
it is trying to plug the holy wound
in my bowels with wrong addresses?
listen let us have death back
when we need him the lost mother
of bliss will sing in the back
seat for you let us come back
with our s.s. and our own banks
this time and for the corpses
compilers to start out dear concerned
chosen esteemed sufferer warm
gloves god our bodies ladders
lovely look we smile too this
way look our blood too touch us is
it horrible? touch us

HOUNDING MERCY

our poor angel how sick
he must be of burying his face
in our hot cunty mouths breathing
in maggots and fruity lung tissue
puffing us up when all we do
is empty again the prayers
to the forbidden father stinking
on us like exhaust fumes the candles
stuck guttering in our backsides
suppose though we took your gun in one
hand your excellent scalpel behind
it and kept saying kiss kiss kiss kiss
and before they screamed we'd cut
them before they begged us blast
them and cannibalize them all legs
from one ethics from another somebody's
skull we'd suture until there was
one whole one and who'd need war
or politics would the mothers kill
their beautiful children from sheer
boredom the fathers fight
over the fucked carcasses like sharks?
here is my magic briefcase
which roars here the branch
of my life to beat it with my
handcuffs what will I want now? give
me love give me snow oceans don't speak

WHAT DID THE MAN DO WITH THE CLOUDS?

the grandmas are all coming down like f-101's like gulls
screaming HAPPIER! HAPPIER! the grandmas
loom along the parapets like old wars their
grooved bellies grenades the lines kissed
into their faces like barbed wire
grandmas I've got the wings you brought me but they won't work
for me they don't fit anywhere on me
except in my mouth I keep sticking them
onto me like matchbooks but brother adam moses the pope
I don't see anyone the grandmas are all laughing
on the back fence like cold soup grandmas
if I could I'd wind myself onto you like a ribbon
and flow out behind you and be wind be sunrise
the grandmas bagpipe out of their soft wombs like apples
and go up like autumn in long rows like pearls like pearls
good-bye grandmas good-bye again thanks
for my present I swallowed them they're flapping
around inside me like uncle sol in the last chair
maybe someday they'll lift me like you
by the top of my guts out of here good-bye
charlie! go to sleep! eat! you're skin and bones! good-bye!
  good-bye!

THE MATTER

there's no no like money's
money makes big holes behind its eyes
when it says no and death
is the next teller
counting you money arches
and peeks down at the caseworker in the spirit drawer
money comes takes your picture without cameras
digs inside without shovels
smiles puts its head in the tube
like a robber
like the anchorite in the cave
like ten dollars
inside money is no candy but her
inside money no rate but just him
the prostitute without her vagina the brother
who wants you to money says no
and the last dollar
which is our friend dog
our history like a condom
lion
king
speaker
is dragged under and riveted
to the bone
like old age

REFUGE, SERPENT-RIDERS

a man decided once to go steal truth
all day he would tie himself to his bed
and not listen
at night the ropes would come off
he would go out and open his mouth
tasting what leaked through the moon from the next sky
rolling the stars around in his teeth
like little pits
finally darkness got tired of hanging there
it said how much will you give me? give me
something
the man started getting younger when he heard that
soon he was crawling the rocks
cut his knees he was really sorry
everybody else screamed BEAST FIEND MURDERER!
they pissed up into his maw
they named their lips death
so when they cried it would break in two pieces
then darkness went back
the stories still hid inside him it was morning
nobody had him
he still knew everything

FLAT

the pillows are going insane
they are like shells the skulls have risen out of them like locusts
leaving faces in them but cold vacant immobile
heavy with tears
they are like clouds and are so sick of us
so furious with us they swear next time
when we come back if they can they will spring up and our
    faces will empty
next time they will soar like clouds and dissolve
and not touch us it is morning
our heads thrown back in agony

the pillows are going insane
from the grief of being laid down
and having to stare unquestioningly like flowers
and be in all places like flowers each man one in his house
one in his barracks in his jail cell
they swear if they weren't going insane they would call to each
    other
like flowers and spring up and come closer
but they must stay quietly
they must have faces like men and wait like men
the dead casings the filling and emptying going insane

THE ADMIRAL FAN

FOR TOM PALMORE

"The imagination of man's heart is evil from his youth . . ."

behind the barn the lady from the city
hikes her girdle up over her white backside
and into her before she knows it all the cows go all
the sheep the chickens geese old mule nannygoat
then o my god all over her breasts so many breasts
we have to make dolls to empty her
but the lobbyist of the dolls would come in his long car
wouldn't he? they are using her in washington
the country gets thin like an old woman
and they are bringing her back to me blubbering
armfuls ripped fabrics bubbles she is sobbing
against me my wife my
nation
the breasts were
dawn amity peace exaltation
in the fields the corn withering tomato vine bean vine
nothingness nothingness this
we flash upon like stoplights

III

"Magnificent! Magnificent!
No one knows the final word.
The ocean bed is on fire.
Out of the void leap wooden lambs."

THE NICKNAME OF HELL

the president of my country his face flushed
horribly like a penis is walking through
the schoolyard toward my daughter I tell him
mr president I will make it all right but
under his hand his penis is lined with many
buttons I tell him the orders are changing
but commanders deep in his penis prime it
I tell him about love I tell him there
is a new god who believes anything I
cringe alongside him I dance like a daughter
it is the schoolyard the daughters play
on the dangerous fences I tell him I love
him I tell him the daughters aren't here
even he is holding me now his arms hold
me his lips you are my bliss he tells me
these are my arms these my lips you
are my penis he tells me his face stings
into mine like a penis you are my joy you
my daughter hold me my daughter my daughter

THE KINGDOM OF STINKING WISHES

how is it some of us don't believe
about evil that it's only a little
of it you're not supposed to get
wrought up poor babies we
never heard mommy telling us
inside we heard her piss fizzing
like champagne but no secrets
and the daddies poor babies
what did they know all scurvied
up like underwear from working
so hard they heard the heroes
scrabbling under their shields
like roaches they heard the gold
coming up but us we keep
running around with band-aids we
can't understand how the judge
could be such an old fart we keep
scratching it we smear the spermy
gook on we kiss it we say there
there and everyone is laughing
and laughing the rich people
cracking pearls in their stomachs
the hungry people licking plain
stones they're hysterical they say
there there babies there there
there poor babies

BAD MOUTH

FOR W. S. MERWIN

not bad mouth
in bad mouth
you know how to beat women so they love you afterwards
and come crawling
how to torture whole races and next time they fight
on the same side as you the lamb out of you
bad mouth lives in three houses with scabbards
bad mouth has hurt since the dinosaurs
even his sperm hurts
like napalm
bad mouth thinking
who do I kill?
who lock up in my arms for the last moment? pity
me pity me

good mouth I want to be vile enough for us both
so we'll love more
I want scorpion ladies I want beautiful pain ladies
and wolf brothers to lick their clear breasts with
good mouth worshiping
good mouth wreathing his genes like fuses
good mouth
I want being able to say help me
help me good mouth
the ones down to the raisin like my tongue
are my tongue the last ones before peace
are inside me
good mouth whoever I let live murdered me whoever I pitied
    burned
please stop me

THIS DAY

probably death fits all right in the world
but every time somebody dies his mother
botches it suddenly she thinks there's not
enough room in her breasts the nipples
are clogged she says the ducts jammed rifles even
so old they sag like laundry she grabs
them and hangs on she doesn't understand she
says she can't understand it mother what
I'm doing is truth mother understand
me at least freedom but o god she can't find
space for an atom her glands burst her
pores swell like bad fruit mother when
we were wolves remember? she doesn't
understand the inside of bodies the voids
wasted the patient holes used up
like planets when I count three she says
everything was a dream everything before
now was really dead was I really dead?

$100,000

how does the judge get pleasure sending
you up so quickly kill him send
him away how does he live what
fun is there in the club judge?
what fun is there in the yellow pain to live here?
judge judge what fun
in the long hunger in the policeman crazing himself
what fun here peeking out from the skirts
the kid holding his ears and his father
somebody goes up to the judge but he's all gone
somebody plays hide-and-seek with his parchments
but he drifts from his scrotum drools
out through the hole in his shoe like great happiness
judge in the gun barrel in the bullet
ticked on the machine in the pause
what fun judge when we're not bitten
in the bail going to heaven like an angel
in the sentence by the word by the dollar
judge in the corner
in the ceiling in the windowpane like an explosion
fun in the hole in the chest loneliness
in the bag over the dead generation
in the chain and self-righteousness
the judge sleeping
the judge born in new innocence
digs around in his own death like despair
goes half-dead like a steer in killed pieces
right wrong coming cleansed like a sparrow
what fun all dead what fun all
perfect then poor dog then father harrow!
him!

THE LONG BELLS

dream please
no favors
your last one
the wings closing the spirit lady the blue
was too much for me
I'd like not to know things like that anymore I'm
not superman it hurts me
I'd like to live in a cigarette advertisement
I'd like to just walk out
and beat my belly like a drum
until they scratched my name off
dream
I want to get dark like you
I want to live with the people named star who get worn down
to the moon by jump ropes and being unfolded
is there anything that would come through like a mountain
and look and go back and take that long I want that one
I have never said no more
dream
but I am now
no more please no more
I mean it

THE RABBIT FIGHTS FOR HIS LIFE THE LEOPARD
EATS LUNCH

FOR HARVEY FINKLE

what if the revolution comes and I'm in it and my job
is to murder a child accidentally
or afterwards to get rid of the policemen?
I had a milkshake last week with a policeman
we talked about his pay raise it eats shit
he told me what if I have that one? SAVAGE
the baby was easy
the baby went up in thin air
I remembered in dostoevsky where they talked
about whether it would all be worth the death of one child
and you decided yes or no according to your character
my character
is how he got back in his car
like a tired businessman and listened to the radio
for a few minutes
and waved
is having to lug him everywhere
I go because I can't take him to his wife crying like this
the children have learned to throw their arms around you
without meaning it to kiss you without feeling it
to know there is something marvelous
and not pay attention
in order to say any of this at all to you
I have made myself up like somebody
in a novel
in order not
to go out of my mind I make it I can only do two things
hold you
bury you

FOR CHILDREN WHEN THEY GROW UP

god is simpler than you are
he's like the one carrying bricks
or you can make girls out of him there is a huge cunt it devours
   you
you lean back you say SAY SOMETHING
you say LOVE ME YOU ARE LIKE HITLER
YOU ARE A ZERO I CAN SEE THROUGH and you see through
the freezing bodies the mouths ashes
I don't remember what else

god I don't remember what else
it was about how easy it is an up and a down?
dying and being born backwards
and having to come in backwards?
god is like one wing he is one hand
I'm so lonely
god so
broken

CRACKS

FOR GLORIA MILGROM

big mercy and little mercy big mercy
eats people they're like governments they can't sleep it cracks
them like toy cars they are this little they're on fire
so little mercy
spits the last drop on them they sizzle off like butter
you're big mercy I'm little it doesn't matter
I'm going to make love to you like a radio
I'm going to make things out of you and sell them back
to you so you'll be the same but some cheaper
then
little mercy says you look nice don't be sad
I'm big mercy now I drag by like a battle I want
not hitting you when you weren't kind I want if I loved you
saying is it different?
then truth comes for a long time
so you don't have to start anywhere people go in jail and then
    out people
hungry people in the crazy house big mercy
is in there his hand is named sparrow
she talks to his hand
in her lap
like a little dog it looks up
what about suicide in the red?
what about living in one valve and remembering?
little mercy lines up in its places you kiss them you
hold on so tight they start choking you can't stop they keep
    choking
on the other side
is who you would marry berserk
from gentleness
and in the house in the field in the last country
wild

CELLOPHANE

if only we weren't so small next to the stars
we could refuse absolutely to be alive in this eon
to be alive now you can't understand one thing without pain
you can't feel your own face in the morning
without wanting to blow up
if we were bigger
we wouldn't keep happening over and over
like truth that hurts worse than anything
with NO big as the mint
and DO IT filling the air like soot from the incinerator
we'd be as easy as the game war
the wingspan from one death to another
and the centuries the unending centuries
taken away from us in cattle cars
would wail harmlessly
like ghosts

THE RAMPAGE

a baby got here once who before
he was all the way out and could already feel the hindu
pain inside him and the hebrew and the iliad
decided he was never going to stop crying no matter what
until they did something he wasn't going
to turn the horror
off in their fat sentences
and in the light bulb how much murder to get light
and in the walls agony agony for the bricks for the glaze
he was going to keep screaming
until they made death little like he was
and loved him too and sent
him back to undo all this
and it happened
he kept screaming he scared them he saw them
filling with womblight again like stadiums
he saw the tears sucked back into the story the smiles
opening like sandwiches
so he stopped
and looked up and said all right
it's better now
I'm hungry now I want just to sleep
and they let him

INCHES

it would be wonderful to be quiet now
to creak down through the fossils making my last speech
into the blind rocks
or to hang from the bars by my belt
and not speak of us our bellows of helplessness our disgust
to be as silent as planets
even the wind has been burned out
hospitals jails the places learning to be hard like men
something where we would be taken and dispirited
of all things like god to godhead love
in peace
not to have "of" to our deaths anymore
the political would go into the back
it would bury itself in itself
and cry for us
I remember you you were my friend I loved you
very much of it was not for words

CRAWL

the bottom of the universe and
cock-monster and piggy we
are crying for each other
we are stumbling out to go
work cock-monster the kiss so
everything but the skin melts
and you are sucked out piggy
flattening on the scum
like a rubber the girl
peeling an orange the doctor
dragging his shoelaces
like flesh cock-monster
in the eighth world I will kill
you with my vagina I
will roast you on the spit
of my forehead piggy
nothing's for sale is
it? except us? no more
flowers fruit the bitter
leaves underneath us we
are sown in the dark
back of death but even us
do you know really?

THE STING

the not want
jesus
I didn't know this the not want
for woman country daughter the man
hit rocked back crying holding him
the not want
for wounding myself for your mouth
for what my hand is opening getting sleepy
the not want
to ride hooked in you like a thistle
for long grass the earth broken to take breaths
in you
jesus
not want
for dreaming
to be president
to take the whole nation and kiss it
awake being born being desired
not new minds not even not
this grown into the big
and fuller
not want
for being able to not want
for trees taking me underneath clouds
taking me fury
exaltation
why? why baby? why dog? why wife?
why
not want president?
why not want friend with no anguish?
why
angel I love you god I love you why
not want heart in my body in each hand

picture guitar
holy
leave this
let this be here
let me
not want this not

THE LAST

when I was sleeping this morning one of my feet
fell out of the covers and my daughter
came in and covered it up with her little dolly blanket

I was dreaming right then that flames were shooting out of my
  cock
and when I woke up with her patting the soft cloth down on me
I believed I understood the end of eternity for the first time

don't ever make me explain this

IV

IN THE HEART OF THE BEAST

IN THE HEART OF THE BEAST

May 1970: Cambodia, Kent State, Jackson State

1.
this is fresh meat right mr nixon?

this is even sweeter than mickey schwerner or fred hampton
   right?
even more tender than the cherokee nation or guatemala or
   greece
having their asses straightened for them isn't it?

this is none of your oriental imitation
this is iowa corn grown
this is jersey tomato grown
washington salmon maryland crab
this is from children
who'd barely begun ingesting corruption
the bodies floating belly up like polluted fish in cambodia
barely tainting them
the black kids blown up in their churches
hardly souring them
their torments were so meager
they still thought about life
still struggled with urgency
and compassion
so
tender

2.
I'm sorry

I don't want to hear anymore that the innocent farmer in ohio on
   guard duty means well but is fucked up by his politicians and
   raises his rifle out of some primal fear for his own life and his
   family's and that he hates niggers hates them hates them because
   he is warped and deceived by events

67

and pulls the trigger

I'm sorry I don't want to forgive him anymore
I don't want to say he didn't know what he was doing
because he knew what he was doing
because he didn't pull the trigger once and run away screaming
they kept shooting the kids said
we thought they were blanks but they kept shooting and shooting
we were so scared

I don't want to forgive the bricklayer from akron who might or
    might not hate his mother I don't care or the lawyer or gas
    station attendant from cleveland who may or may not have had
    a bad childhood
I don't care
I don't want to know
I don't want to hear anything about it

another kid said the rocks weren't even reaching them!

I don't want to understand why they did it

how could you?
just that

everything else is pure shit

3.

on the front page of the times a girl is screaming
she will be screaming forever
and her friend will lie there forever you wouldn't know she
    wasn't just sleeping in the sun except for the other screaming

and on the editorial page
"the tragic nature of the division of the country . . . the provocation
    undoubtedly was great and was also unpardonable . . ."

o my god
my god

if there was a way to purify the world who would be left?
there is a list
and it says
this person for doing this
and that person for doing nothing
and this person for not howling in rage
and that for desperately hanging onto the reasons the reasons
and this list
there is an avenger
who would be left?
who is there now who isn't completely insane from all this?
who didn't dream with me last night
of burning everything destroying everyone
of tearing pieces of your own body off
of coughing your language up and spitting it away like vomit
of wanting to start at the bottom of your house
breaking everything floor by floor
burning the pictures
tearing the mattresses up
smashing windows and chairs until nothing is left
and then the cars with a sledgehammer
the markets
the stores that sell things
the buses
the bridges into the city
the airports
the international harbors
the tall buildings crumpling like corpses
the theaters torn down to the bare stage
the galleries naked the bookstores like mouths open

there should be funerals in front of the white house
bones in the capitol

where do you stop?

how can we be like this?

4.

I remember what it was to come downstairs
and my daughter would be there crawling toward me as fast as
    she could
crying HI DADDA HI DADDA

and what it was to bury my face in my wife's breasts and forget

to touch a friend's shoulder
to laugh
to take walks

5.

I don't want to call anyone pig

meeting people who tell you they want war they hate communists
or somebody who'll say they hate niggers spics kikes
and you still don't believe they're beyond knowing
because you feel comfortable with them even drawn to them
and know somehow that they have salvageable hearts
you try to keep hope
for a community that could contain both of you
so that you'd both be generous and loving
and find ways that didn't need hatred and killing
to burn off the inarticulate human rage at having to die

I thought if I could take somebody like that in my arms
I could convince them that everyone was alone before death
but love saved us from living our lives reflexively with death

that it could happen
we would be naked now

we'd change now little by little
we'd be better
we would just be here
in this life

but it could be a delusion couldn't it?
it could be like thinking those soldiers were shooting blanks
up until the last second standing there scared shitless
but inside
thinking americans don't shoot innocent people!
I know it!
I learned it in school in the movies!
it doesn't happen like this
and hearing a bullet slam into the ground next to you and the
    flesh
and every voice in your body saying o no no
and seeing your friend go down
half her head blown away
and the image of kennedy in back of the car
and of king
and the other kennedy
and wanting to explode o no no no no no

6.

not to be loaded up under the flopping bladewash the tubes sucking
    to be thrown out turning to flame burning on trees on grass on
    skin burning lips away breasts away genitals arms legs buttocks
not to be torn out of the pack jammed in the chamber belched out
    laid over the ground like a live fence of despair
not to fog down into the river where the fish die into the rice
    where the frogs die into the trees where the fruit dies the grain
    dies the leaves into the genes

into the generations

more black children
more red children
and yellow

not to be screaming